Birds & Beasts
AFRICA

FOR EMMA AND JOE

BRYAN HANLON

Birds & Beasts
AFRICA

OBSERVATIONS
OF A
WILDLIFE ARTIST

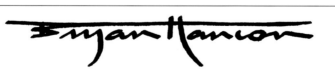

SWAN·HILL
PRESS

Acknowledgements

The Author wishes to thank: –

COUNT KONRAD GOESS-SAURAU, without whose help, encouragement and interest in Africa and its wildlife, this project would never have happened. Thank you for making it possible.

PAUL SPICER – Lonhro Plc, and all management and staff of Lonhro Hotels, Kenya Ltd, who made my stay with them so comfortable and problem free.

CHARLES DOBIE, (T. D. Dobie & Sons) (Tanzania) for the lifelong memories acquired at Mbuyu Camp in the Selous Game Reserve and at Raskutani on the coast.

HENRY NDEDE (ELSAMERE CONSERVATION TRUST) Niavasha, at the spearhead of conservation education.

ROD HALL, MBE. – BRITISH AIRWAYS ASSISTING NATURE CONSERVATION for his thoughts, ideas and all his work for conservation world-wide.

RENÉ HALLER – Bayobab Farm, (Portland Cement) Bamburi, Mombassa, a true conservationist and visionary. Thank you for showing me your project and the wonderful accommodation on the beach.

TED GOSS, EADEN WILDLIFE TRUST, NAIROBI, for the informative time spent in the Shimba Hills.

WILLY AND SUE ROBERTS, MASAI MARA, for the loan of the Land Rover, allowing me to explore the Mara at will.

KEVIN PILGRIM (BALLOON PILOT) and wife Sarah, for looking after me in the Mara and those enchanting balloon flights.

JOHN AND JANET NOBLE, (OL'PEJETA RANCH), for the loan of the Range Rover, affording me independence for a few days and allowing me to explore the local Bush.

CBM VISUAL COMMUNICATION LTD, SWINDON, to all the management and staff for their patience, friendly service and high standard of work.

PATRICK PAPE (CAMPING SAFARIS), for the wonderful but all too short stay at his camp and the long walk in the Mara with his knowledgeable and friendly Masai guides.

MARY HILLIER, for her hard work and tenacity in sorting out and typing up my notes.

L.A. BENNUN – HEAD OF ORNITHOLOGY, NATIONAL MUSEUMS OF KENYA, NAIROBI

I would also like to mention the following, all of whom have added knowledge, friendship and pleasure to my adventures:
Paola Bordoni, Guido Bernardinelli, Marco Villa, Paul and Val Mettem, William Kikanai Pere, Abubakar A. Shee, Joyce Poole, Daniel T. Haller, Dr Ludwig C. Frits, Mohamed Ismail, Mike McDowell, William and Camilla Sheppee, Eddie and Jenny Matthews, Ken and Norma Selvester, Primrose Stobbs Sal, Dr Colin Forbes, Ian and Jane Craig, Tibor Gaal, Michael Lenaimado.

Copyright © 1997 Bryan Hanlon

First published in the UK in 1997
by Swan Hill Press, an imprint of Airlife Publishing Ltd

British Library Cataloguing-in Publication Data
A catalogue record for this book
is available from the British Library

ISBN 1 85310 363 2

Typeset by Phoenix Typesetting, Ilkley, West Yorkshire.
Printed in Hong Kong.

Swan Hill Press
an imprint of Airlife Publishing Ltd
101 Longden Road, Shrewsbury, SY3 9EB, England.

Introduction

It was a sweltering hot day at the 1990 Welsh Game Fair. Everybody was in the refreshment tents or relaxing in the shade, the aisles between the exhibitors being relatively void of life. I noticed a tent promoting the latest Rodger McPhail book. Partly from curiosity and partly to escape the heat I wandered in; the occupants were smartly, if somewhat inappropriately, dressed for the weather. I struck up a casual conversation with a man who turned out to be the managing director of the publishing company responsible for this book.

I finally got around to mentioning that I was an artist specializing in natural history subjects and would he mind if I sent him some slides of my work. He accepted my offer, I thanked him, said goodbye and emerged into the searing heat, feeling a slight sense of achievement and positive about our brief encounter.

When I received the reply to the selection of slides that I had sent, I was sitting on the edge of my bed. It was a beautiful sunny spring morning and the birds were singing, but I had a feeling of doom and despondency. Fearing the worst, I opened the letter. Imagine my delight, surprise and almost shock, because not only did he like my work, but wanted a meeting at our earliest convenience, to view the paintings and discuss ideas for a possible book project. Well, it could have been the dreariest day in mid January, but for me, it could only have been spring, the blossoming of new life, the start of a new era.

Given an opportunity like this, what does one do? I have been interested in and have drawn and painted birds since being a small boy, and have recently expanded my repertoire to include mammals and landscapes to produce paintings that contain all three, but where was the theme for the book?

I was discussing the developments with a friend, Rod Hall, MBE, a British Airways engineer and creator of BAANC 'British Airways Assisting Nature Conservation' a small organisation within BA dedicated to aiding conservation projects world-wide by providing transport and promoting education and responsible tourism. We discussed and mulled over many ideas before Rod came up with a suggestion 'Island Wildlife'. 'What do you mean?' I said. 'Well' he said, 'take six or seven groups of islands around the world, visit them, paint, draw and make notes on the flora and fauna, and any current conservation projects, and do a chapter on each location.' 'What sort of islands?' I said. 'Well,' he replied, 'you could start at Pribilof Island in Alaska, then maybe Scotland, say St. Kilda, through to the Med. Maybe Aride Island in the Seychelles, Fothergill Island in Lake Kariba Zimbabwe, then on down to Heron Island on the Great Barrier Reef, Australia.' I sat with mouth ajar and an expression between wonderment and bewilderment. Rod was familiar with many of the places he mentioned and I knew that he was serious!

For a wildlife artist, what I was hearing was almost unbelievable – a dream. We settled on that idea and spent the next few months sorting out details, itinerary, destinations, travel timescale, etc. I prepared a synopsis to persuade the publisher on the merits of such a project.

I did not have long to wait for the verdict: 'Great, wonderful, . . . but!' There is always a but. 'Two small problems.' 'First – these places all seem to be obscure, unheard of, not popular or well known.' 'Yes, well I could not argue with that.' 'Secondly' – 'you as an artist, well, you are not exactly a household name are you?' 'Well, no, I suppose not,' came my humble reply. Then they pointed out that having two negatives is not a good start. 'However, what about Fothergill? You know Fothergill Island in Lake Kariba, that is Africa isn't it? Everybody knows Africa and its wildlife, so stick with Africa – that is positive.' 'OK then' I muttered.

I relayed their feelings to Rod and although disappointed, he suggested it was better than a total rejection and that we could do the 'Island' book next time.

I could not believe my luck and good fortune. As a relatively unknown artist I had approached a publisher and secured a contract to produce a book about my work on African subjects.

It was at a 'cooler' subsequent Game Fair that I approached Europe's Premier Wildlife Gallery (The Tryon), with whom I have been associated. It was with great enthusiasm and anticipation that I explained to one of the Directors (David Bigham), my good fortune and plans for the project. He asked if I had been to Africa, 'No' was my reply, 'Ah well,' he said, 'you have to know Africa to do Africa' . . . Somewhat deflated I looked for the nearest refreshment tent to console myself and ponder my predicament.

Seated under a massive parkland oak, surrounded by all the familiarities of a midsummer country event, the fact that I had not been to Africa before meant I had few preconceived ideas. I could go with a clear train of thought, a blank canvas and be receptive to all I encountered and then free to interpret in whichever way felt honest and true. I finished that drink feeling reassured and more confident about the path that lay ahead.

Although the publisher and British Airways were in agreement that the project should go ahead, I did not have sufficient funds or appropriate contacts to make a substantial trip to Africa possible.

Time slipped by and little progress was being made with regards to the trip and the work that would result. I was beginning to feel anxious. It was not until a few months later, with the deadline looming and still no progress, that I began to panic. It was now a 'do or die' situation and in a state of desperation I decided to contact a local gentleman, (Konrad Goess-Saurau), who had been introduced to me by a mutual friend, David Margesson, a year or so earlier. He in turn became a friend and supporter of my work. I had known that he had spent several years working in Africa, during which time he had travelled widely on safaris.

We arranged a meeting at which I outlined my situation and concerns regarding the project. He listened intently and commented enthusiastically. I remember our parting, a handshake and his comment 'Don't worry, we will do it!' and do it he did. Within a few days he had made several contacts, enquiries, and arranged a meeting with Paul Spicer of Lonrho Plc, which at that time had several hotels and safari lodges in Kenya. Within weeks we had a three-month trip sketched out. July and August in Kenya, September in Tanzania. New life and hope had been restored because without his intervention, enthusiasm and support the project was in grave danger of fading beyond redemption.

The paintings and sketches in this book, although gleaned from observations made over a three-month period, represent a tiny fraction of what was possible. The surface film on a sandy river pool or a tick on a buffalo's hide, are but two examples of ideas that create the proverbial grain of rice on a checkers board. I physically have produced enough work for one book, but mentally I have enough for many volumes. I have tried to steer clear of the conventional African genre, having no previous experiences or influences. I have tried to paint as open-mindedly and receptively as one can and to paint only subjects that truly excite me.

I remember showing a selection of my works to a print publisher. Several of them featured skulls, dead animals and the odd grotesque bird. 'Well, you do not compromise' was his comment, to which I replied 'I certainly hope not', somewhat flippantly of course. One does compromise, there is no alternative, life is a compromise. It is the degree that is important. I have many ideas involving the portrayal of dead, half-eaten, dried and decaying carcasses, bleached bones and matted hair, all such a feature of the African plains. They were the things that said so much to me, not just about Africa, but life, death and the cycle of being. The carcasses scattered about the plains emphasize the primeval purity, a testament to the history and solidity of a place that has witnessed the re-enactment of these dramas millions of times in the past and will bear witness to many millions in the future, God willing. Each carcass representing sustenance for countless predators and scavengers, a link in the food chain, even providing new life to the parched earth where they lay, through the nutrients leaching from their decaying forms.

In contrast to these images, I encountered many incidents containing great beauty. A jacaranda tree in full bloom brightening up a Nairobi suburb; the bougainvillaea bushes, flowering aloes and many more, their colour, beauty and frailness accentuated by their harsh surroundings.

Birds were constant companions, bringing vibrant colour and animation to any scene; kingfishers, rollers, starlings, sunbirds and bee-eaters being some of the most striking and regularly encountered. Butterflies, dragonflies, beetles and spiders, of many varying shapes, lizards and geckos, the list goes on.

For one interested in natural history with an observant eye, there was a kaleidoscope of colour, a point of interest at every turn, in every situation, the opportunities too numerous to record, too unpredictable to relax. An example:

We had spent an active afternoon in the wooded hills around the Shimba Hills Lodge, setting out goats to attract leopards. It was now getting dark and we were in the bar chewing biltong and discussing the merits of the afternoon forays. A moth came in, attracted by the light and was caught in a spider's web. Immediately a gecko shot out from between beams to snatch it from the spider, as it did so a bat appeared from the open window and attempted to claim the moth from the gecko. A short but vigorous tussle ensued, ending with the bat flying back from whence it came and the gecko returning to his lair to consume his prize. This three to four second incident happened just feet away on the ceiling. The other guests in the bar were being entertained by a pair of bush babies, helping themselves to peanuts and drinks and were oblivious to the drama. This is a typical example of what can happen at any time. I will probably never find a way of directly using this incident in a painting but the memory will stay with me for a long time and will manifest itself through my work in other ways.

I hope that by viewing my pictures and reading the text in this book you are able to share in some of the moments of sheer wonderment and delight that I experienced during my three months of observation in East Africa.

Eland Mother and Calf
(Taurotragus oryx)

Baobab Farm, Bamburi, Kenya.

9" × 13" (229 × 330mm) Tempera on Arches

Although eland seem to be numerous on the plains of East Africa and are
encountered frequently, they also seem to be one of the most shy antelopes, seldom
allowing the viewer to approach closer than a few hundred metres – most
frustrating!

It was not until I visited Baobab Farm, Bamburi, just north of Mombasa that I
could get close to a resident herd that was being 'farmed' there, and I was able to
observe these impressive beasts at close quarters.

René Haller, the man responsible for the Baobab Project, pointed out to me that
the dominant animal in the herd makes a 'clicking' sound with its front knee joints
as a means of keeping in contact with the other herd members in dense
undergrowth and particularly at night. I witnessed this myself while sketching the
animals just a few metres away.

The animals I have painted (mother and calf) stood motionless, apart from the
occasional shake of the head, twitch of the ears and swish of the tail, with the calf
gently nuzzling its mother in the afternoon sun. This endearing scene lasted for
about twenty minutes, allowing ample time for sketching and notes.

The scene was made all the more attractive by the quality of the
light caused by the low angles and warm
tones of the setting sun.

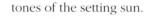

Mangrove Melange

Bamburi, Kenya.

11" × 14" (279 × 356mm) Oil on Canvas

As the sun filtered through the canopy causing a melange of light, shade, form and pattern, I reflected on what the scene must have been like not that many years ago, when the whole coastline was fringed with mangrove and before the holiday homes and hotel chains set up camp.

   The idea for this painting came from observing two very small remnants of mangrove outside the chalet in which I was staying as a guest of Portland Cement, Bamburi.

   I toyed with the idea of placing some hotels in the 'pool' of light between the boughs, but preferred the sense of space in contrast to the tangled foreground.

   The bird I chose to add interest and a spot of colour was an obvious one, a mangrove kingfisher, one of three or four members of the same family with very similar colouring of blue, grey and red. The mangrove kingfisher is distinguished from the others by its all-red bill.

Heron and Hippo

Selous Game Reserve, Tanzania.

(Hippopotamus amphibius)

24″ ˘ 18″ (610 ˘ 457mm) Oil on Canvas

It was a perfect morning; the sun was bright and clear, the air fresh and scented, the temperature comfortable for shorts and T-shirt, and I was full of anticipation for what the day had to offer – my favourite time of day. Breakfast had just finished, most of the guests had gone on a game drive and it seemed as if I was the only one left in camp. I took my coffee, sketchbook and binoculars to my favourite seat on the patio, from where I could survey the river and beyond. It was about this time that the bird-table was topped up with fruit left over from breakfast. The resident bird population knew this too and were gathering in the nearby trees and shrubs in anticipation, providing me with a wonderful opportunity to sketch and take notes.

The scene out in front was fairly typical, with hippos and crocodiles in the shallows, wading birds of many types stalking the edge, kingfishers hunting in the small pools – malachites from over hanging branches, pied kingfishers hovering in flight. Buffalo emerged from the scrub on the far bank and a couple of bush pigs were at the water's edge. A fish eagle punctuated the cacophony of birdsong that filled the air at this time of day with its evocative call. It was heaven!

However, my attention was taken by the antics of some ground squirrels, four of them playing around a hippo skull on the river bank. One was feeding on palm nuts while the others chased about, using the skull to hide in. One sat in the eye socket for some time eating a piece of nut.

I was becoming absorbed with the scene when suddenly the squirrels disappeared in all directions. There was a whoosh of wings, and with a bouncy landing a grey heron alighted nearby. After surveying the area for possible danger, it ambled over to the skull for a closer look, prodding and poking it with its massive bill. When it was satisfied that all was well, it stepped up onto it and began to relax. After a short spell of preening it slumped into its 'sunbathing' pose, which I had witnessed and sketched for the first time just weeks before at Baobab Farm, Bamburi, Kenya. It seemed at one with itself and its surroundings.

While frantically sketching and making notes of this rather bizarre sculptural form, I noticed a movement by the skull, now in shadow from the cradled wings of the bird. I gently raised my binoculars for a closer look. To my delight and surprise it was one of the squirrels emerging through the eye socket, where it had sought refuge minutes before. It settled itself down in the shade before continuing its meal.

It is these magical moments that make watching nature so exciting, never knowing what is going to happen next. I can only think that if the heron had noticed the squirrel, it could have become a meal itself, rather than just resuming one.

The whole blissful episode ended in a frantic flapping of wings and a dash back into the skull. A member of staff came onto the scene to top up the bird-table. I had my notes and sketches and an indelible impression in my mind for I knew this was a painting I would have to do. The episode left me with a feeling of joy and fulfilment – and it was still only 9.30 am.
feeling of joy and fulfilment – and it was
still only 9.30 am.

Marabou Stork Resting
(Leptoptilos crumeniferus)

Sweetwaters Camp, Ol'Pejeta Ranch Kenya.

20″ × 16″ (508 × 406mm) Oil on Canvas

When people see these birds, the words ugly and grotesque are used frequently to describe them, which is understandable. But the plumage of the marabou stork can be very handsome, with its slate-blue/grey back, darker wing feathers edged in white, white neck ruff and underparts, and white powder puff under the tail, all providing a very smart attire. Combine this with its hunched posture, slow but purposeful gait and it reminds me of a smart old gentleman at a funeral. In contrast, the bare skin areas around the head and neck are very vivid in colour, particularly in the breeding season. The pink-red face and sac, cerulean blue nape and vermilion neck 'bladder' all provide the artist with a wealth of interest and challenges which I found hard to resist. It was pure self-indulgence!

I had many opportunities to observe these birds at close quarters as they used the waterhole outside my tent at Sweetwaters Camp. They would arrive around mid-morning, after presumably having eaten somewhere, and would stay for the rest of the day, sleeping, preening and generally relaxing. It was not until late afternoon that their activities increased. As the temperature and sun began to fall, they would react with each other and squabbles would break out, with a clapping of bills and flapping of wings. They also showed great interest in objects around them, picking them up and rearranging them. One individual spent a leisurely half-hour tossing lumps of elephant dung and sometimes catching them!

As these antics subsided the birds prepared themselves for the short flight over the tents to the tall yellow acacias which they would use for their roost. Gathering at one end of the 'runway', each in turn would run the 25–30 metres into the wind before taking off, swinging sharp-right, low over the tents. Their large size, the rush of air through their primaries and their closeness as they passed over the tents made for an exciting finalé to the afternoon's observations.

While going for a stroll just before dark on a particularly windy night I saw these storks in their roosting trees. They were on the highest and most peripheral branches; the branches did not look substantial enough to bear their huge forms and swayed to and fro, the birds looking as if they were on a roller coaster. How did they hang on with those ungainly feet? They looked so vulnerable, their dark silhouettes swaying frantically this way and that against the darkening sky with the moonlit clouds racing behind. I could not think of a more precarious and uncomfortable place to spend a night. However, since they rest and sleep most of the day, perhaps they do not need to sleep at night.

They were all there the next day, seemingly none the worse for their experience.

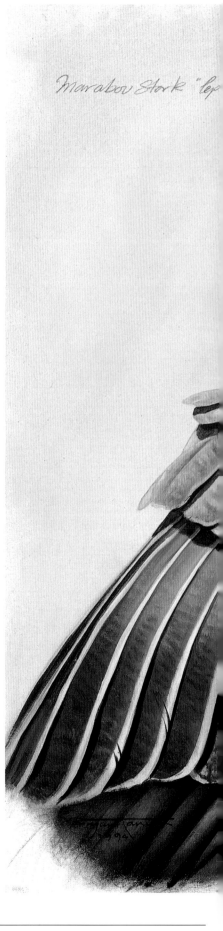

Rock Hyrax and Purple Grenadier
(*Heterohyrax brucei and Uraeginthus ianthinogaster*)

Hell's Gate National Park, Naivasha, Kenya.

8½" × 11½" (216 × 292mm) Watercolour

I first encountered hyraxes at a picnic spot called Baboon Rock, an outcrop overlooking Lake Nakuru with its thousands of flamingoes. They were used to visitors and would solicit titbits from tourists, but they would have to compete with the resident agarmi lizards when the food was thrown down. I made several sketches and notes which I worked up later in the studio.

It was not until I came across them again in Hell's Gate National Park that I was able to utilize those sketches. They seemed more timid here and I was unable to draw them in the way I would have liked, but what made the scene more interesting was a pair of purple grenadiers, beautifully coloured little finches, which were enjoying the sun with the hyrax.

I have not yet come up with a satisfactory composition for a full painting, so I made this studio sketch for future reference while the image was still clear in my mind. There has to be a wonderful picture; all the ingredients are there – the endearing hyrax, slightly toy-like, with its soft muted colours juxtaposed with the bright garb of the sharp and sprightly grenadiers picked out in the bright sun and set against the dark shadowy areas of the caves and crevices amongst the rocks.

RPLE GRENADIER.
aeginthus ianthinogastar.

ck HYRAX.
terohyrax brucei"

lls Gate G.P. Naivasha
Kenya. 93.

1995.

Anticipation

Selous Game Reserve, Tanzania.

12″ × 17½″ (305 × 444mm) Tempera on Arches

I was sitting on a small clifftop observing the to-ing and fro-ing of a colony of white-fronted bee-eaters over the fast-receding water of Manze Lake, a tributary to the mighty Rufiji River. A movement in the surface scum attracted the attention of a green-backed heron which I had not noticed before. The scum concealed something lurking beneath; was it a fish, a frog or a crocodile? As the heron moved stealthily towards the movement just below the surface, I wondered if it was about to catch a meal or become one? The continuous saga of life and death was about to be re-enacted.

The sand rivers and tributaries of the Selous Game Reserve, Tanzania, are rapidly drying up, concentrating fish, frogs, crocodiles and birds into ever-diminishing pools and all looking to feed off one another.

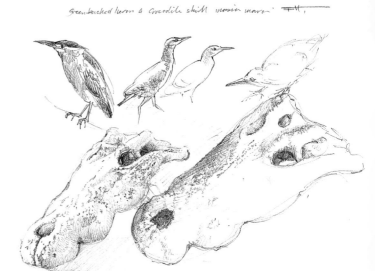

Migration Past

Masai Mara, Kenya.

16″ × 20″ (406 × 508mm) Oil on Canvas

Bones collect in eddies and backwaters, reminding one of the times just past when the food was plentiful, and for crocodiles, lions and other predators the living was easy. Then, the restricting crossing places along the Mara River were heaving arteries of wildebeest and zebra.

The seasons move on and as the waters recede along with one's memory, the exposed and bleached bones act as a reminder of the frantic panic and commotion, noise, dust and mud created by thousands of beasts having to run the gauntlet and cross a river in order to reach fresh pasture.

The scene I have chosen to paint is in stark contrast, one of peace and quiet, as a heron stalks the receding water's edge in search of a meal on a lesser scale. As it steps across the crocodile, one is reminded that it is not only the hoofed masses that are vulnerable; the big and powerful can also fall in these dramas.

Bateleur Eagle
(Terathopius ecaudatus)

Masai Mara, Kenya.

19" × 26" (480 × 660mm) Tempora on Arches

My intention when starting this picture was to produce an interesting image, one that concentrated on design, composition and the dramatic effect of strong directional light on the bird's powerful head. I had no intention of producing a full painting.

After drawing the three subjects my idea was to paint in full the bird on the right, the head and neck of the left-hand bird and maybe a light wash on the bird crouching between the two, with a lot of white paper and graphite – an exercise in form and colour, with no thought of knurled branches, distant landscapes or stormy skies.

However as the work progressed, I found myself being dictated to and compelled to paint more, so it did not stop with the three birds; I found the background beckoning, and my original ideas flew out of the window. I thought at one stage that I had lost it and was about to give up. I had a struggle to stay in touch, and even when the painting was finished I was still not convinced. But, all my doubts were finally dispelled when I saw the picture framed months later; it not only expressed some of my original ideas regarding design but it also showed a great deal of dramatic power.

Wattled Crane
(Bugeranus carunculatus)

12" × 9" (305 × 229mm)

Acrylic on board

Although I was familiar only with the pelican in Africa, I have included the other two birds because of their similarity in artistic format and 'feel'. To me they are all very much of an entity, an exercise in form, texture, light and shade. Composition also playing an important role; they could almost be simple abstract forms within the confines of their own space.

   This was a self-indulgent exercise, and one which gave me great satisfaction. It was the first of many pictures in which I concentrated on the main subject, filling the frame and arranging it in an interesting and pleasing way to try to get depth into a relatively shallow space.

Pelican
(Pelicanus onocrotulus)

Acrylic on board

7½" × 12" (190 × 305mm)

Down to the River (Buffaloes and Bee-Eaters)

Mara River, Masai Mara

Oil on Canvas 14" × 20" (356 × 508mm)

Even in the Masai Mara there were times when the game viewing is less than exciting. It was at such times that I found myself gravitating to the river and exploring its banks, with the added dimension of water and the numerous nooks and crannies found between its meanders, there was always a chance of something unexpected to enlighten an uneventful afternoon.

I would find a vantage point, usually by the side of one of the many crossing places used by the herds at migration time and by all game as convenient access points to the water's edge. Apart from these 'slipways' the majority of the river is edged by steep banks which are unsuitable and under-cut in places, making access to the river dangerous. However, the slipways used are also precarious, being favoured by the larger predators as places to ambush thirsty visitors.

On this occasion, apart from the obligatory hippos resting in the pools, the joy of the afternoon came from a small family group of little bee-eaters, the parent seemed to be doing most of the fetching and carrying, joined by the youngsters when impatience got the better of their caution. They must have just fledged, and reminded me of young swallows at home fresh out of the nest.

The only other animals to visit were a small group of very wary buffaloes, they shuffled around, seemingly afraid to approach the water's edge. Whether it was my presence or something else disturbing them I never found out, as darkness fell I packed up my sketch-book and made my way back to the Lodge.

Giraffe
(Giraffa camelopardalis)

13" × 19" (330 × 483mm) Watercolour

No matter what a giraffe is doing, be it resting in the shade, browsing on an acacia, sparring with its neighbours or galloping flat out across the plains, it seems to be completely relaxed, as if all its movements are in slow motion. They appear to be so graceful and gentle, but this impression can be deceptive; their kick is a formidable weapon and deterrent to even the largest of predators.

While at Ol'Pejeta Ranch I met John and Janet Noble, who had a baby giraffe called Jemima, an orphan they had cared for. When feeding her it was easy to see how giraffes' muzzles and tongues worked; they are fine, dexterous and marshmallow soft, but it was difficult to see how they managed to pick tiny green shoots from between the wicked acacia thorns without causing themselves harm.

I watched a young giraffe come down to the water in the heat of the day for a drink. After several unsuccessful attempts and a lapse of 20 minutes or so it finally succumbed to its fear and caution and returned thirsty to the bush. The tension in that animal was obvious for the duration of its stay by the river, a delicate battle between its vulnerability and its need to satisfy its thirst.

It probably made the right decision; a day or two later, returning from a game drive we came across an unfortunate mature giraffe near the same spot, wandering around in a state of shock and confusion. One could only imagine by the nature of its injuries that it had been attacked by a crocodile as it had attempted to drink. It looked as if it had been seized by the lower jaw and had thrown its head back to try to shake off the reptile. All the skin on the bottom half of its head from below the ears had been torn and was hanging from its lower lip, swaying from side to side as the poor animal wandered aimlessly.

I sketched the image as soon as I was back in camp, and went to sleep that night with it in my head and the roar of lions and the cackle of hyenas in my ears.

Nature was left to run its course and the giraffe was not seen again.

"Tazga" masai mara

Heron's Repose

Baobab Farm, Bamburi, Kenya.

19" × 26" (483 × 660mm) Tempera on Arches

There were several of these birds relaxing on an island just a few metres away, with crocodiles and tilarpia in the water, kingfishers hunting and displaying, and yellow and black male weaver birds hanging from their nests suspended from branches overhanging the lake, doing their best to attract partners. I was on the patio area having a cold drink and crocodile kebab – most welcome after a morning spent exploring the area in the hot sun. I could sympathize with the herons dozing in the heat of the day in their angelic poses.

The situation was perfect, sitting in the shade with, in front of me, the ideal models to sketch. This was the first time I had seen herons adopting this pose, although I did see it again at Mbuyu Camp in the Selous Game Reserve, Tanzania. I used the notes and sketches made here at Baobab Farm for the painting (opposite) and on page 13.

I found it somewhat comforting to be so far from home yet drawing such a familiar bird as the grey heron, the same bird as found in Europe. These moments of familiarity occurred periodically from the evocative calls of curlews, sandpipers and plovers on the coast, to one of my favourite bird songs – that of the willow warbler. I heard this on many occasions while exploring the woods, scrub and papyrus shores of Lake Mombasa. There is something very reassuring about a familiar sound amongst all the exotic ones of the African bush.

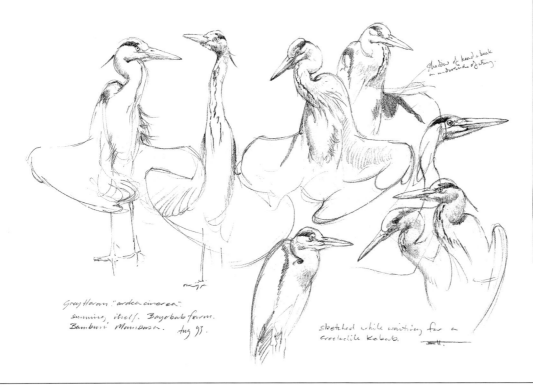

bari, Mombasa. Kenya.

My First Lions
(Panthera leo)

Masai Mara, Kenya.

16" × 20" (406 × 508mm) Oil on Canvas

I remember reading an article in the *SWARA* Magazine by Jonathan Scott, a renowned wildlife photographer and author, in which he said if he could only have one day in Africa he would spend it in the Masai Mara. After returning in the early evening from my first game drive in the Mara I could fully understand his sentiment.

I had been in Kenya for about a month and had seen and experienced many wonderful and exciting moments from the flamingoes of Lake Nakuru to the lichen-laden woods and their inhabitants of the Aberdare Mountains, but it was not until I reached the Masai Mara with its fenceless vistas, blue escarpments, meandering river and plethora of wildlife that I sampled the Africa of my dreams.

Returning to my tent, trying to recall what I had seen that afternoon was a challenge – there had been so much: a cheetah with cubs, hyenas and vultures squabbling over the remains of a wildebeest. I had also seen zebra, giraffe, buffalo, several species of antelope, a bat-eared fox, jackals. Birdlife included storks, vultures, eagles, bustards, ostrich, ground hornbills and secretary birds. A myriad of passerines of all shapes, sizes, colours and habits had caught my eye and there were also geckos, lizards, snakes, insects, butterflies, beetles . . .

As if I had not had enough, on the way back to the Mara Safari Club, with the sun sinking low, there by a small stream was a pride of lions (my first) quenching their thirsts and being playful between their afternoon's slumbering and evening's hunting. We watched as they satisfied themselves before melting into the evening; I was enthralled, enchanted, bewildered.

I sat on the verandah of my tent overlooking the Mara River watching the moon's reflection in its dark waters. Hippos grunted and snorted, an owl hooted and the cicadas and frogs added to the cacophony of sounds that were so perfect an end to my first day in that magical place and what was probably the most complete afternoon's game-watching of the trip.
And I had another three more weeks of it –
could I cope?

my first lion (simba) massai mara   Aug 93

Bryan Hanlon
1993

Bee-Eaters and Buffalo
(Merops oreobates and Syncerus caffer)

The Ark, Aberdare National Park, Kenya.

18" × 24" (457 × 610mm) Oil on Canvas

Disappointment was my first reaction as we made our way along an elevated walkway to the Ark. I arrived with high hopes and expectations, owing to glowing reports of the game-viewing opportunities that it offered. I was disappointed because, being mid-July and the middle of Kenya's winter, the area was shrouded in low cloud, fog and mist, which restricted viewing to a few metres.

The Ark is a wonderful wooden building set on the edge of a forest clearing overlooking a waterhole and mineral lick in the heart of the Aberdare Mountains, with terraces and balconies inside and out, and a ground-level dugout all offering excellent game-viewing, weather permitting. My time there was short, and as the weather showed no sign of improving I settled down to make the most of the animals I could see – buffalo, waterbuck, Egyptian geese and cinnamon-chested bee-eaters amongst others.

Despite the fog and mist and the limited selection of wildlife, the sketches and notes I made during my short stay resulted in, if not the most successful paintings, certainly some of the most popular. The ambience created by the fog and mist, with the animals appearing and disappearing like ghostly figures, softened the whole scene, offering a pleasant contrast to days of bright sun and harsh light.

The cinnamon-chested bee-eaters were a wonder to watch. They would huddle together as if sheltering from the damp and then one would fly off into the abyss and return moments later with a butterfly or other insect – I could hardly see the birds in those conditions let alone the insect!

Buffalo and Yellow-Billed Oxpeckers
(Syncerus caffer and Buphagus africanus)

Masai Mara, Kenya

16" × 20" (406 × 508mm) Oil on Canvas

This 'portrait' (opposite, top) was the first of several depicting buffalo in similar poses and varying mediums. When watching them in the wild it is easy to see how they have acquired their reputation for being powerful, bad-tempered and dangerous, particularly if they are in a group of bachelor males.

As a subject for painting I found them most inviting. Their massive bulk and form enveloped in a dry, crusty rather threadbare hide, their formidable horns, knobbly and knurled at the base going through to shiny black and polished at the points, and their small beady eyes give the animal an air of menace – a challenging exercise.

On viewing the finished picture weeks later I realised that I had left the birds out. Buffalo and other large game frequently have egrets and oxpeckers in attendance.

The buffalo I encountered had yellow-billed oxpeckers as constant companions. The animation of their brightly coloured yellow and red beaks are in stark contrast to the dull grey-brown of their hosts. Rather than add the birds to a picture I had finished weeks before I decided to treat it as a preliminary work and start afresh using the knowledge I had gained.

After a lot of deliberation and head-scratching, I decided on a less menacing-looking female staring straight out with the birds and their brightly coloured beaks adding interest and zest.

I sometimes wonder whether a bird flying out of the picture towards the bottom left-hand corner would have added to the dynamics of the piece – maybe next time.

Buffalo Portrait
(Syncerus caffer)

Masai Mara, Kenya

8" × 10" (203 × 254mm) Watercolour

Fish Eagles
(Heliacetus vocifer)

(Opposite top)

Rusinga Island, Lake Victoria, Tanzania.

9" × 12 ½" (230 × 330mm) Tempora on Arches

During my brief stay on Rusinga Island I had a wonderful opportunity to observe these magnificent birds at close quarters. There was a large fig tree in the garden, with not only two or three very large hamerkops nests, but at the top, an occupied eagle's nest with a fully-fledged youngster. The way it regularly exercised its wings told me it was not far off leaving. Unfortunately the great size of the tree and the arrangement of its large leaves made observing the nest difficult.

Lake Victoria and the much smaller and shrinking Lake Naivasha have some of the highest densities of fish eagles in Africa; it was at the latter that I found the time and opportunity to study them at length.

Elsamere,
Lake Naivasha
8" × 12" (203 × 305mm)
Watercolour on Arches

Elsamere, the home of the late George and Joy Adams who both met their fate in tragic and violent circumstances, is now not only a hostelry for the responsible-minded tourist but one of the major conservation and educational establishments in Kenya, guided by the very capable Henry Ndede. It was while staying there that I first experienced the true African dawn chorus; not only was I periodically woken by the munching sound of hippos grazing the lawns outside my hut, but I would wake every morning, first to the calls of the resident troop of black and white colobus monkeys (which are very rare around the lake as they normally live at higher altitudes), closely followed by one of the most evocative sounds of the African bush – the fish eagle. Add the pure call of the tropical bulbul and my emotions and imagination were truly inspired.

The picture shows two birds taking a break from the chores of parenthood and relaxing on a large fig tree bough in which they have their nest, but both aware of an intruder violating their air space.

Fish Eagle
and Osprey
*8 ½" × 12 ½"
(215 × 320mm)
Tempora on
paper*

Fish Eagle +
Osprey -
Creator Lake
Nr Lake Naivasha
Kenya - November 91.

Successful Suitor

Masai Mara, Kenya.

20" × 16" (508 × 406mm) Oil on Panel

I had several encounters with this particular male lion, whom I named Al after Al Capone. He was always on his own and looked slightly forlorn, instantly recognisable by his badly scarred face. I assumed that he had been fighting with other lions and had been cast out. I had not seen him for a few days and was beginning to wonder if he had suffered another attack and either been driven further away or worse.

There was subdued excitement over breakfast at the Mara Safari Club one morning; a group on the early game drive had come across a pair of 'honeymooning' lions – when lions pair up they go off together for several days, seeking solitude and privacy. Their habit of mating on a regular basis, about every 20 minutes or so throughout the day and night make them a must for the tour guides.

Later, on the way back from an afternoon excursion, with the sun fading and a full moon rising with the promise of a beautiful evening, I came across the happy couple out in the open, very near the track. Imagine my surprise and delight when, looking through binoculars, I recognised the male as Al. My view of him changed; instead of being forlorn and outcast he was now the successful suitor. I suspect that he acquired his injuries competing for his partner's affections.

I made some frantic sketches as the light was almost gone, wished them luck and made my way back to the camp. It was while bumping along that I decided that a portrait of him was in order to commemorate the event. He is portrayed in the full light of day, but set against the onset of night with the stars and a full moon illuminating the heavens as befits such an occasion.

Young Lion Resting
(Panthera leo)

Masai Mara, Kenya.

10" × 12" (254 × 305mm) Oil on Canvas

When I look at these two paintings and the field sketches, I am transported back to a blissful Mara afternoon in the company of a small group of lions all enjoying an after-lunch siesta. The scene was typical, with some of the adult females lying on their backs, legs in the air – very unladylike – and others sprawled over boulders; even the cubs were inactive, lying motionless with swollen bellies and contented expressions. A large male was away from the main group and partly concealed by scrub and thick grass. Apart from the odd waggle of an ear, sweep of a tail and twitch of a muscle to discourage flies, they were quite still – surely only the 'King of Beasts' can afford to relax in such a way.

When viewing lions in this sleepy state it is hard to think of their other side. Only the remains of their last kill reminds one of the tremendous activity and drama, the speed, power, strength and violence that had occurred just hours before and countless times before that.

It was early afternoon and all was quiet; there was no bird song, just the occasional butterfly and the hum of insects to break the quiet, still heat of the afternoon.

I had the afternoon and the lions to myself, I settled down to what was one of the most absorbing and rewarding afternoon's sketching sessions of my life.

Young Lion Dozing
(Panthera leo)

Masai Mara, Kenya

10" × 12" (254 × 305mm) Oil on Canvas

Morani, The Black Rhino
(Diceros bicornis)

Ol'Pejeta Ranch, Kenya.

19" × 26" (483 × 660mm) Tempera on Arches

Morani was a black rhino who lost his mother to poachers. He was hand-reared from an early age and although several attempts were made to reintroduce him into the wild, all proved unsuccessful. He never got on with the wild resident population of rhinos; they would chase and sometimes attack him. The last time he was attacked he narrowly escaped with his life and had to be recaptured and brought into care.

He now lives in his own 20-acre compound with a full-time guard. His past experiences must have seriously affected him, for when he catches the scent of a rhino investigating the perimeter fence of his compound, he cowers like a scolded dog and hides in a log corral. Morani is Swahili for 'young warrior', which is not very apt. He was however a great model as both black and white rhinos eluded me in the wild; it was only animals involved in rehabilitation programmes that afforded me the opportunity to observe them at close quarters. There was Morani at Ol'Pejeta and a pair of white rhinos in the Masai Mara.

I managed to spend some time with Morani on two occasions; he was tame enough to stroke and pat, but one had to be aware of his horn as he tossed his head about occasionally. On my first sketching session some alfalfa was put down to keep him in one place; things were going well until something spooked him and, with a grunt and a snort he came bowling over to me. I jumped up and looked for the guard, who had a rude awakening from his afternoon nap. I left him to calm Morani down, which he did with a few words in Swahili and a pat on his back, but not before Morani had managed to toss my stool in the air. I thanked the guard and we exchanged reassuring smiles. I retrieved my stool and resumed work, but somehow things were not the same – my heart was still thumping. It is not every sketching session where one is confronted by a 'young warrior'.

There was talk of producing a number of prints from the painting I was to make of Morani, the proceeds of which could help with the running costs of the project. This seemed to influence my ideas about the work; I did not find it easy to settle on any one pose and in the end I decided on a montage with Mount Kenya in the background – on a good day one could see the mountain from his enclosure. Because marabou storks were very prominent in and around that area I included them, ominously circling as they would with vultures over dead game, to signify the vulnerability and plight of the rhino in Africa. The yellow-billed stork was added to introduce a cheerful bit of colour, a ray of hope.

Waterbuck
(Kobus ellipsiprymnus)

Masai Mara, Kenya

19½" × 26" (495 × 660mm) Tempera on Arches

Waterbuck, although handsome beasts, seem to be slightly incongruous on the open plains. I remember watching them at the Ark in the Aberdare National Park; it was foggy, damp and cold, and they were in and out of thick reedy vegetation bordering a waterhole shrouded in mist. With their thick, somewhat shabby coats, they seemed well-suited to the situation and at home.

In contrast, down on the vast plains where I spent many a hot afternoon, they seemed out of place. I cannot imagine why they have such thick coats, when all the other plain's game have short ones. However, this was a particularly handsome specimen, with large even horns and a coat, which though long-haired and thick, was in pristine condition.

I have painted two versions of the same animal so that I could show the two different markings on the rear end, the lower one showing the typical 'target' of a white circle on the rump around the tail and the other more common version of an all-whitish rump.

Waterbuck ♂
"Kobus ellipsiprymnus"

Masai Mara Aug 93.

N.B. showing different rump markings

Not out of the Woods

Masai Mara, Kenya.

18" × 24" (457 × 610mm) Oil on Canvas

I stopped to observe and sketch this jewel of a bird, perched on the remains of a Masai *boma*, its colours flashing as it preened in the midday sun, neon-like against the dark shadowy wood behind. Lilac-breasted rollers are common in areas where the habitat is suitable, and they are quite obvious because of their habit of finding prominent perches – telegraph poles or wires, dead trees, etc. – from which they survey the surrounding area for food. Because of their familiarity it would be easy to take them for granted, which would be a great shame as they are one of most colourful birds encountered.

It was not until the roller flew off in a panic that I noticed the movement of an elephant's ear; I was so intent on the bird that I had not noticed a small group of elephants camouflaged by foliage and dappled light. It was one of the magical and impromptu moments that abound in the Mara. There and then I decided to record the event on canvas, taking rough notes and sketches to assist my work in the studio. It was a revelation to see how quiet, gentle and unobtrusive animals of such size and bulk can be.

Although I came to Africa with few preconceived ideas, it was exactly this situation I was hoping to encounter.

Chimpanzee, Starling and Sparrow
(Pan troglodytes and Spreo superbus)

Ol'Pejeta Ranch, Kenya.

18" × 13" (457 × 330mm) Watercolour and Bodycolour

Chimpanzees are not natives of East Africa, this one was part of a small group who were to be initial members of a rehabilitation and study centre which was being set up at Ol'Pejeta Ranch, Kenya. The man in charge of the project, Vince, showed me around the site where the enclosures were being built. They took in several acres of bush and woodland and have a river running through them; they looked impressive and I wish the venture the best of luck.

The chimpanzees' native homelands of Central and West Africa were considered too dangerous for such a project, as poaching and the killing of them for food by local people is still a major problem.

I sketched this one as it relaxed below me. I was concentrating on the facial features, intending to do a portrait and not concern myself with its body. However I found the black mass of fur was a means of framing the face and contrasting its features.

I included the starling and the sparrow as one associates these birds with humans and chimpanzees are about as human as animals get. The cigarette butt was discarded by his mate who, I was told, has become quite addicted to them; it is the first thing she asks for by going through the motions of smoking one and then holding out her hand whenever she sees a visitor.

Chimpanzee (Pan troglodytes)
Superb Starling and Rufus sparrow
Kenya 93

Chimp, Starling, and Sparrow,
(Sweet waters tented camp.)

Nonchalant

Masai Mara, Kenya.

20" × 30" (508 × 762mm) Oil on Canvas

This was my first serious attempt at a full African landscape. I chose Masai Mara as it was familiar and typical of the savannah lands, with wide open spaces stretching as far as the eye could see towards the distant Aitong Hills.

I have admired many a landscape and panoramic view in many places, but never really felt the urge to portray them in paint, always focusing on what the landscape was made up of and what it contained, particularly the flora and fauna. But in Africa I felt the need to portray the environment for its own sake, first by doing small water-colour sketches and then by building on them.

The experience triggered something and I know that landscapes and environment will progressively feature in my work. I see it as a natural progression, broadening one's horizons and taking in the whole. It is no good saving a single species if the habitat is no longer there or not of the right quality to support it.

I kept the bottom two thirds of the picture subdued and with little contrast to emphasise the mood and to accentuate the sun illuminating the distant horizon. The lion has no interest in the zebra and the zebra very little interest in the lion, to the extent that one has even turned his back on him. It is typical of how predator and prey instinctively read one another's moods.

Beauty and the Beast

Masai Mara, Kenya

8" × 10" (203 × 254mm) Oil on Board

As I have always been interested in birds and drawn and painted them from an early age, I found it difficult to ignore them when selecting subject matter for this project.

One can spend many hours game-watching and not see a mammal, but one would be hard pushed to spend any time anywhere and not see a bird; they are a constant source of interest and enjoyment. There were several small birds occupying the thicket of whistling thorns above the dozing lion, probably female weavers or sparrows, but I chose this more picturesque variable sunbird, not just because they are one of my favourite birds and always in and around the garden, but because they are a thrill to draw and paint. It is not often one gets the chance to use such a spectrum of colour; I had to be careful, as they could have featured in all the pictures.

old scareface: snoozing in the mid day sun. Masai Mara Aug 93.

The Ark

Aberdare National Park, Kenya.

20" × 30" (508 × 762mm) Oil on Canvas

As with the painting 'Bee-eaters and Buffalo' (pages 32-33) this picture was conceived during my 24-hour stay at the Ark. One of the characters that kept us entertained on that dreary afternoon was a male Egyptian goose. He was jealously guarding his mate and would run flapping his wings and honking at anything that got too close. Like the bee-eaters, he seemed to be able to see in the fog; he would react most strongly to other incoming geese well before they came into view, and if they did not heed his warnings and presumed to land, he would be onto them in an instant, giving them no quarter and making them wish they had heeded his warning.

The young waterbuck was attracted by his antics and sauntered over under the watchful eye of his mother.

Waterbuck and Egyptian Geese
(*Kobus ellipsiprymnus and Alopochen aegyptiacus*)

Masai Mara, Kenya

10" × 12" (254 × 305mm) Oil on Unprimed Canvas

As a preliminary sketch with the colours and tones involved, I decided to use unprimed canvas. Its neutral tone and texture were helpful to the subject matter; in fact, I was surprised at the minimal amount of paint I used for the effect, allowing the canvas to do a lot of the work in the way I would allow the white of the paper to show through in a watercolour. I was pleasantly surprised with the result, and intend to use it more often!

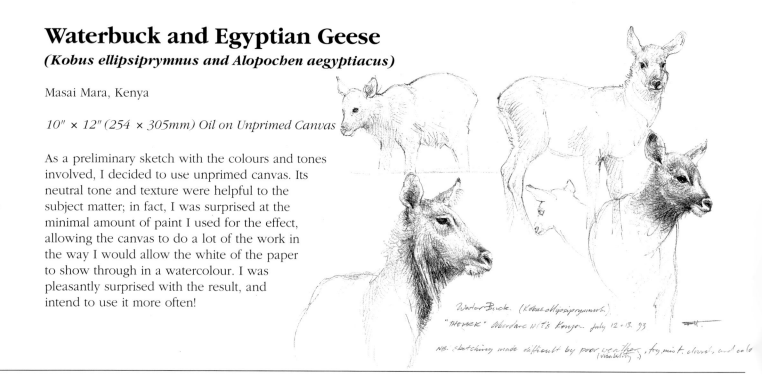

Barn Owl and Gazelle
(Tyto alba and Gazella thomsoni)

Masai Mara, Kenya.

16" × 30" (406 × 762mm) Oil on Canvas

From a European's point of view this situation may at first seem a little incongruous – a barn owl in the Masai Mara in the company of antelopes. But although they are localised, they do occur in the Mara and many other parts of East and Central Africa. In fact, as owls go, they are spread the world over and are found on most continents.

While painting the dead treestump I was thinking of what bird to put on it. If it had been a European scene an owl would have been an obvious choice, but it did not seem appropriate for the plains of Africa until I was talking to the local 'birdman', who happened to mention that he had seen barn owls on several occasions, mainly whilst travelling across the Mara at night. Day sightings are rare and only happen when the parent birds are pushed to find enough food for their brood.

I did manage to see one, and it was during the day. I was on a plane at Mombasa airport bound for Dar es Salaam, Tanzania; we were taxying when I noticed some distance ahead on the side of the runway, a cream-white bundle animated by the wind. As we accelerated towards it my suspicions were confirmed, it was a barn owl, which had probably been struck early that morning. Their habit of hunting by quartering the ground low, makes them vulnerable not only to road traffic but, it seems, to aeroplanes too.

Thomson's Gazelle
(Gazella thomsoni)

Masai Mara, Kenya.

9" × 12" (229 × 305mm) Tempera on Arches

Although 'tommies' are among the most numerous antelopes of the plains and are encountered daily, I did not tire of them, always finding them a joy to watch. In the Masai Mara they were very tame and I could sketch them at leisure; the ones here were sketched from a topless Land-Rover kindly lent to me by Willy Roberts, Head Ranger for this area of the Mara. It was such a relief to have my own transport and please myself where I could go and for how long I could stay.

There is something very African about a herd of 'tommies' delicately nibbling their way across the plains, their busy tails and gentle natures belying their alertness to the ever-present threat of attack as they seem to be the lunchbox of every predator on the plains and in the air.

I recall one morning when the plains seemed deserted, apart from a young prancing 'tommy' and a jackal doggedly pursuing it. The two were meandering across the open space parallel to one another, and every now and then the jackal would rush in causing the 'tommy' to panic. As these attacks became more frequent and the gap narrowed the 'tommy' realised that it was in serious danger. The somewhat playful bravado ceased as the chase hotted up and the pair disappeared over a rise in the ground to continue their survival game in the next valley – I have often pondered the outcome

Pied Kingfisher
(Ceryle rudis)

Ras Katani, Tanzania.

8″ × 10″ (208 × 504mm) Oil on Canvas

Ras Katani was an idyllic camp set on the beach overlooking the Indian Ocean, with virgin sands stretching north and south as far as the eye could see and not another camp anywhere. A few native fishermen foraged for squid and fish amongst the coral at low tide.

The location was isolated and blissfully peaceful, in complete contrast from the hurly burly of Dar es Salaam, where I had previously been. What was truly unique about this setting was a freshwater lagoon beside the camp which drained over the beach and into the ocean; it added another dimension to the area, attracting freshwater species of plants, fish and birds, complementing the seafaring species.

The vegetation around the lagoon was lush and teeming with life. Kingfishers used the numerous perches to rest and hunt from while hamerkops and herons stalked the shallows, dragonflies took insects, butterflies frequented flowers and monkeys chased around in the overhanging treetops.

Life and Death

Masai Mara, Kenya

14" × 14" (356 × 356mm) Oil on Canvas

When we arrived at this scene, the dust was settling. The cheetah was panting heavily, its whole body expanding and contracting, testament to the effort expended in securing its prey. The Thomson's gazelle gave a few frantic kicks before expiring, its head flopping heavily to the ground as the throat hold was released. The cheetah collapsed, it did not have the strength to eat until it had rested for a good ten minutes.

It is a scene that takes many forms and is re-enacted the world over, be it a spider catching a fly, a cat catching a mouse or a whale sifting creel, but nowhere can it be so obvious and so apparent as on the plains of Africa. If one does not witness an actual kill, the reminders of previous encounters are scattered about the savannah in varying degrees of decay, including bleached bones and dried hides.

In these circumstances life and death are one, co-existing; it is therefore fitting, that a painting depicting such a subject be included in this collection.

Calm after the Storm

Masai Mara, Kenya

8½" × 12½" (216 × 318mm) Tempera on Arches

All was calm as our truck drew to a halt, a tranquil scene belying the activity and mayhem just an hour or so before. The dust had settled, and all that remained of what must have been quite a gathering were two or three vultures, a jackal and a couple of hyenas looking full and reluctant to move away from the ever-cautious jackal. What little remained of the wildebeest was still fresh and only emphasised how narrowly I had missed the real action.

The opportunity to witness such a primeval scene, where a gathering of assorted predators and scavengers snarled and scratched out their hierarchy while squabbling over a common food source excited me. It was so very African, so very untamed.

Masai Mara, Kenya.

Young Buffalo and Crowned Plover
(Syncerus caffer and Vavellus coronatus)

22" × 24" (559 × 610mm) Oil on Canvas

I am often asked which out of all the pictures I have completed for this project I am most pleased with. I have tried to make them as diverse and cover as broad a spectrum as possible, so a favourite is difficult to choose, but this one of buffalo would be high on the list. I cannot explain why this one appeals to me; it may be the handling of the landscape, which has been substituted by the patchwork of bodies, giving an interesting backdrop for the young animal. Although the texture of the calves' bright ginger-red fur, made all the more striking contrasted against the dull brown-grey of the adults, was a challenge, it was one which I found most satisfying, and I consider the result a success. The format too, being almost square, seems to suit the bulk and form of the animals, with the crowned plovers giving an added interest and focal point, not only for the young buffalo but also for the viewer.

Kudu and Starling
(Tragelaphus strepsiceros and Spreo superbus)

Selous Game Reserve, Tanzania.

10" × 12" (254 × 305mm) Oil on Canvas

This small picture was one of the first where I chose the landscape for its colour and texture, a screen or backdrop for the kudu to mingle with. Depth was important but not distance. The foreground, with its props of aloes and elephant dung act as the stage, a path leading to the eye of the kudu with the movement and contrasting colour coming from the superb starlings.

Glossy Starlings gathered
in the trees around me
as I sketched the
Greater Kudu.

Selous Game Reserve
Tanzania. (September).

their plumage shone like sweet wrapped from a
Christmas selection box!

Cheetah and Balloon (Controversy)
(Acinonyx jubatus)

Masai Mara, Kenya.

18" × 24" (457 × 610mm) Oil on Canvas

The inspiration for this picture did not come from the landscape, the cheetah nor the balloon and the glamour associated with such a mode of game-viewing, but from the controversy and debate caused whenever a balloon operation is set up.

During my stay at the Mara Safari Club I met an interesting man. Kevin Pilgrim, a balloon pilot from Canada, was there with his wife Sarah and a locally-acquired dog, Zulu, and was running a balloon safari operation based at the Club. We were both interested in similar aspects of the local area – the flora and fauna and the local Masai people, their language, customs and ways – and spent several evenings discussing them.

However, the most controversial subject was the ballooning itself. There is no doubt that silently rising at dawn in a massive, multicoloured balloon which is regularly illuminated from within by a roaring flame is a surreal experience, affording one a unique position from which to view vibrant sunrises. Then to float in whichever direction the breeze takes you, viewing the game beneath, the birds in the treetops and flying by, the all-round vistas, the colour, the landscapes, the long shadows cast by isolated trees as the sun creeps over the horizon, all in an eerie silence, dream-like, punctuated only by a roaring flame needed to maintain level flight is truly memorable. It culminates in a champagne breakfast in the bush, and is an activity few are lucky enough to experience. I consider myself extremely fortunate, therefore, that owing to Kevin's kindness I was given the opportunity to do so, not just once but four times, and the memories will remain with me long into the future.

However, conservation bodies and other interested parties are worried about the amount of disturbance caused to animals by the balloons, in particular the noise. To be effective the balloons have to fly low (called tree-topping) in order to see the game, and to maintain this low viewing position requires regular blasts of the gas, causing a low-frequency roar. Many animals have hearing which is susceptible to low frequency and it is these that are most at risk from the balloon's activities; elephants give particular cause for concern.

I spent some time with Willie Roberts, the Head Ranger for this part of the Mara who was an opponent of the balloon safaris. The dawn was just breaking over his camp in the bush, the bird song was building, the atmosphere was chill and fresh, a more peaceful, isolated spot you could not imagine. Then a muffled roar was heard in the distance, then again, and again at regular intervals, getting louder. This went on for several minutes. It could only be a balloon and as the roar got disturbingly loud I went outside my tent to investigate. The balloon was passing over a few hundred metres to my right, the occupants clearly visible gesturing and waving; Willie was already gesturing back!

Over breakfast Willie explained to me that, because of the position of his camp in relation to the launch site and prevailing winds, six or seven flights out of ten head his way at the most serene time of day, dawn.

I remember at school something about every action having an equal and opposite reaction. Now I had witnessed first-hand the reasons for the controversy.

The picture was painted on separate canvases to represent the two halves of the debate.

Camels and Blackhead Plovers
(Vanellus tectus)

Sweetwaters Tented Camp, Kenya.

36" × 24" (914 × 610mm) Oil on Panel

This painting is one of three that were commissioned for a client in Oman and not painted as part of this project. However, because it was one of the first in which the birds, although not the main point of interest, played an important role in the composition and content of the work, I felt they justified its place here.

Having drawn and painted birds from an early age, I find it difficult not to include them in works which focus on mammals; they are my first love, and the thought of not including them became impossible when I encountered the vast variety that seemed ever-present when I was out game-viewing.

I only encountered camels at Sweetwaters Tented Camp; they had a small herd there which they used for camel trekking. It was a wonderful way of seeing game – quiet, comfortable, elevated and accepted by the wild animals. I was particularly pleased with these two, their position and form, their heads and particularly their muzzles and the coarse matted fur, provided a wealth of challenges in the rendering of subtle texture and fine detail – immensely satisfying when it works, frustrating to say the least when it does not.

Lilac-Breasted Roller
(Coracias caudata)

Masai Mara, Kenya.

9" × 12" (229 × 305mm) Tempera on Arches

We encountered this individual during a game drive with Kevin, the balloon pilot, and his wife Sarah. It was her twenty-fifth birthday and as a treat Kevin arranged some transport (not easy in the Mara) and a picnic. He had heard the migration was heading north and the front-runners were about an hour and a half's drive away across country. They very kindly invited me along and we set off on what turned out to be a very enjoyable excursion.

We found a pleasant spot on the banks of the Mara river on a large bend with rapids downstream, hippos in the pools and weaver birds attending their nests overhanging the water. A small group of three or four little bee-eaters were hawking insects nearby and kept us entertained while having our picnic. What could be more pleasant: perfect weather, wonderful location and company and enough activity for one who is interested in wildlife and art to be absorbed for many an hour.

A small group of bare-faced go-away birds came by, calling and chasing each other from bush to bush, I had seen white-bellied go-away birds many times but these were quite different and special. However it was the lilac-breasted roller that caught my attention. I had often seen these birds, but this one seemed more confident, and allowed me to approach quite close, making notes and sketches. It flew off once or twice to catch insects but returned to the same perch, so I thought it was about time I did a portrait of this striking bird.

Rufous Crowned Roller.
"Coracias naevia"
no streamers.

Lilac Breasted Roller.
"Coracias caudata."

Masai Mara. 93

Zebra
(Equus burchelli)

Hell's Gate National Park, Naivasha, Kenya.

24" × 30" (610 × 762mm) Oil on Panel

I remember the morning when I did this picture very well. I was with Henry Ndede from Elsamere at the gates of Hell's Gate National Park just as the sun was rising over the distant hills. A light covering of cloud was dispersing and the day had promise. We were soon inside the park and on the lookout for anything interesting. The air was cool and fresh and full of herbal scent and the dew on the grass and foliage was heavy and hung in large droplets, the odd one catching the first rays of sun and sparkling. I noticed an early sunbird flying around a bush, looking as if it was drinking from the droplets of dew but I could not be sure.

The area is famous for its vultures; the cliffs and gorges are perfect for them. There was a time when lammergeyers (large, bearded vultures) were seen here on a regular basis, but they have not been seen in recent times. No one seems to know why they have declined – there are a few theories and there has been talk of reintroducing them, but until we understand the reasons for their decline I do not see the point.

A solitary secretary bird was on the lookout for breakfast and illuminated by the sun. It was still too early for the vultures to leave their cliff ledges; they normally wait for the ground to warm up a bit, creating thermals for them to soar on. Insects were starting to move, attracting the attentions of the bee-eaters, and the plains game were also shaking off the chill of the night and becoming more active, with zebra, hartebeest, giraffe and gazelle appearing in greater numbers.

We saw nothing spectacular that morning but it was a memorable occasion.

Down to the River
Eland (Tragelaphus oryx)
Blacksmith Plover (Vanellus tectus)

Mara River, Masai Mara, Kenya

12" × 20" (305 × 508mm) Oil on Canvas

I was not planning to stop at this spot, but as I approached I noticed a small family group of eland making their way to the water's edge.

Eland are one of the more shy antelopes, and this could provide me with a golden opportunity to view them at close quarters. I gave them a wide berth, circling and quietly coming to rest a hundred metres away, turning off the engine; they did not seem to mind my presence and continued unflustered.

The scene was one of peace and tranquility, the mother eland chaperoning the youngster, the calf being distracted by the continual pipping of the plover, a large bull eland already down by the river attended by oxpeckers look back as if to signal the coast was clear and all bathed in a very pleasant mid-morning light.

There were a group of carmine bee-eaters, probably on migration, hawking flies over the river which added colourful animated dimension to the proceedings. The episode lasted twenty minutes or so before the antelope returned to the plains and the bee-eaters moved on, the plover remained quietly picking the water's edge.

Although not dramatic, a God-given moment of blissful peace and one I will cherish for many years.

Elephants and Egrets
(*Loxodonta africana* and *Bubalcus ibis*)

18" × 24" (457 × 610mm) Oil on Canvas

I came across a family group of elephants. They adopted the usual protective, out-of-facing circle with the juveniles finding sanctuary between the legs and trunks of their elders. While observing this mass of blue-grey and beige hides, and the movements of heads, ears, trunks and legs swaying gently and adjusting position, I wondered how to depict the scene without repeating the cliches of 'big game art'. I had the idea of filling the whole canvas with elephant. There had to be a point of interest. The young ones were perfect, being framed themselves by others in the group.

   I saw the smallest of the herd gently nuzzle and caress the tusk of another, larger creature. It was over in a blink but I registered it in my memory and made a sketch. I followed up the sketch with a series of photographs of both the whole group and details of individuals. It was almost a year later, back in my studio that I began to work on the composition.

Elephants and Egrets
(Loxodonta africana and Bubalcus ibis)

10" × 12" (254 × 305mm) Oil on Canvas

I have not had a great deal of luck with elephants in Africa, only coming across them on a few occasions. On one of these occasions it was pointed out to me that one of the young was suckling from its mother, but I could not see it. 'No, no,' said the guide, 'the other end.' I was looking at the rear end, but they suckle from between the front legs – the only animal to do so. I could not believe that something so basic and unusual had escaped my notice, so I thought that a painting was in order, to remind me that there is always another revelation just around the corner, no matter how basic.

I focused in on the main point of the subject, the calf suckling, at the same time creating an interesting design with the elephants' heads and trunks and to give it space and animation a flock of cattle egrets transversing the horizon.

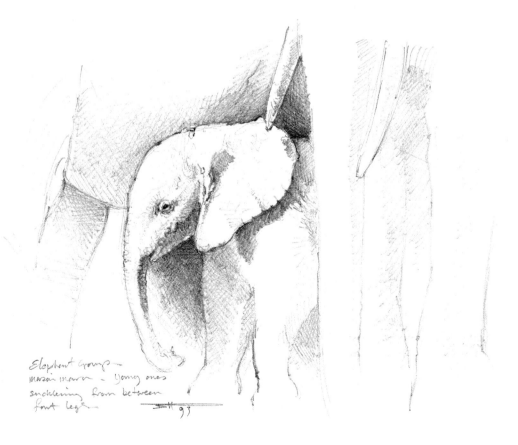

Elephant group –
masai mara – young ones
suckling from between
front legs –

Jambo and Family

36" × 24" (914 × 610mm) Oil on Canvas

This painting was commissioned by the Jersey Wildlife Preservation Trust, the creation of the late, great Gerald Durrell; it formed part of an exhibition to commemorate the Trust's twenty-fifth anniversary.

The models for the gorillas were the impressive Jambo, a magnificent example of a silver-back, one of his wives and a new-born baby.

Jambo was launched into the media limelight when a small boy fell into his enclosure. He lay motionless, knocked unconscious by the fall. Jambo immediately went over and shielded him from the attentions of the more excitable young males; visitors looked on in amazement as Jambo gently stroked the boy's head with apparent tenderness and care while waiting for help. The boy made a full recovery – he has a great story to tell his children backed up by numerous press cuttings and video clips. Jambo himself recently passed away and I am sure will be greatly missed by his keeper, the zoo's staff and all the visitors who knew him.

Gorilla (Jambo + family)

Mara Sundowner (Giraffe)

Masai Mara, Kenya.

15″ × 24″ (380 × 610mm) Oil on Canvas

Although one can marvel at the wonders of sunsets and sunrises, the subtle complexities of tone, colour and form, constantly changing as the day begins and ends. It wasn't until I experienced them regularly on the African equator, particularly when viewed across wide open savannah lands, with the dying sun's rays refracting purple, pink and mauve in the dust clouds kicked up by game traversing these spaces that I was compelled to tackle such a subject.

At first the subject seems simple enough, but one very soon realises the subtleties are complex and difficult to master; it was for this reason that my first attempt (Mara Sundowner) was kept relatively simple, with the sky taking only fifty per cent of the painting as opposed to the normal two thirds, the nuances of colour and form have been kept to a minimum, giving me the chance to keep it under control and opting for the activity to be placed in the foreground: the sacred ibis coming in to roost, the giraffe leaving his supper to rejoin his group on the open plains and the nightjars starting their night-time forays for moths and beetles.

With the completion of this relatively simple painting, the knowledge and confidence I have gained will help me in the future and I am sure this time of day will feature in future landscapes.

Crowned Cranes
(Balearica pavonina)

Baobab Farm, Bamburi, Kenya.

19″ × 26″ (483 × 660mm) Tempera on Arches

It was late afternoon, with the sun sinking, when a pair of crowned cranes pitched into a shallow lake covered in water hyacinths. I had been watching a yellow-billed stork fishing. They attracted my attention as they started to perform, pausing periodically to do some token fishing before resuming their courtship.

I submitted this painting to the world's most prestigious bird art exhibition, held annually at the Leigh Yawkey Woodson Art Museum, Wausau, Wisconsin, USA. To my amazement and good fortune, it was accepted and later reviewed by James Aver, a critic with the *Milwaukee Journal Sentinel*. I quote: '*Crowned Cranes* has much of the insouciant charm of a pair of Ziegfield girls as visualized by Erte.'

One cannot say fairer than that! It was just what I was thinking, as they pranced around on their African stage, illuminated by the limelight of the setting sun.

Crowned Crane
(Balearica regulorum).
Bayobab Farm, Bamburi, Mombasa.
Kenya 93.

CROWNED CRANE
"Balearica regulorum"

Masai Mara Kenya.

The Dawning of a New Day, Cheetah with Tommy
(Acinonyx jubatus and Gazella thomsoni)

Masai Mara, Kenya.

18" × 24" (457 × 610mm) Oil on Canvas

It was not long after starting this picture that I realised its potential, it excited me from the start and by the halfway stage I had come to the conclusion that although the size was pleasing, a larger canvas would be more appropriate for the subject.

Mara Dawn, Cheetah with Tommy

Masai Mara, Kenya.

24" × 48" (610 × 1220mm) Oil on Canvas

I changed the angle of the head, included the whole body, added a cisticola and some guinea-fowl feathers, worked the grassland more intently and drew it on a 24" × 48" canvas, a format new to me. How successful my efforts are I will leave for others to judge, but personally it has given me as much satisfaction as any I can remember.

However, reflecting on the two, I prefer the posture of the first; the angle of the head, its contempt for the viewer giving it presence, arrogance and an inner confidence which seems watered down in the second larger painting, due to its confiding gaze and more relaxed pose.

Cheetah with Cubs
(Acinonyx jubatus)

Masai Mara, Kenya.

18" × 24" (457 × 610mm) Oil on Canvas

This picture was painted almost as an antidote to the two previous ones containing dead gazelles (pages 88-89). I resisted responding to observers' comments and suggestions along the lines of 'What a shame about the gazelle', and 'Why couldn't you paint some cubs in it, they would be much nicer.'

Although it is a perfectly legitimate subject, I have always resisted painting the 'cute and cuddly', the picture with instant appeal for some. However, the comments were persistent, and after a while I began to think about substituting some cubs for the dead gazelle; after all it says as much about Africa as the more 'gruesome' paintings and life is a compromise.

After finishing the picture and showing it to those same people, their reaction was predictable, with comments like 'There you see, that is much nicer' and 'Ah, aren't they lovely, so sweet.' I commented that the cubs were just one side of the coin. 'What do you mean?' I pointed to the canvas on the floor containing the gazelle, 'There is the other side, they co-exist; one cannot survive without the other.' They looked blank, not wishing to spoil the illusion of the 'cute and cuddly'.

I said no more. If conservation is to have a chance then education is the only way; unless people begin to understand the basics of nature, the world and its environment, then one cannot expect them to take it seriously. Sentimentality is a human trait and should not be confused with or substituted for a true understanding of nature.

Buffalo and Secretary Bird
(Syncerus caffer and Sagittarius serpentarius)

Masai Mara, Kenya.

20" × 16" (508 × 406mm) Oil on Canvas

My first encounter with a secretary bird was on an early morning excursion at Hell's Gate National Park. I could not believe how large it was. It looked so majestic, its white breast flushing pink in the rays of the rising sun and its black head-dress standing erect, reminding me of the origins of its name. It was the sole occupant of a vast plain, scanning the ground before it as it strutted in search of an unsuspecting rodent or snake, which it would despatch by stamping on it with its fist-like feet. I watched it for a good 30 minutes as it purposefully meandered across the open space. It paused once in its search to consume a grasshopper or something similar, but had no luck with anything more substantial.

The sketches and notes I made during this period of observation, were used in this picture with the buffalo. The scene portrayed is somewhat more sedate, with neither the bird nor the buffalo looking particularly interested, sitting out the heat of the day.

Owl's Roost
Spotted Eagle Owl (Bubo Africanus)

Mara River, Masai Mara, Kenya.

20″ × 16″ (508 × 406mm) Oil on Canvas

This was a truly wonderful spot, as on many occasions when things were 'slow' on the plains I looked for more productive sites along the river.

This one was better than most, a very pleasant afternoon was spent observing the toing and froing of a selection of life, from the butterflies on the water's edge to the incident depicted in the painting.

It started with a duiker emerging from the bush behind me. I held my breath and daren't move as it daintily tip-toed past my Land-Rover just a metre or two away, and proceeded towards the water. As it approached a tangle of roots and vegetation, a hornbill dropped out of the canopy above and started creating a commotion.

The duiker froze, muscles tense, nerves twitching, ears and eyes scanning for the slightest movement that might pre-empt a predator's attack. What was the most gentle serene moment had without warning turned into one of great angst and tension. A moment or so had passed when the cause of the fuss revealed itself: a large owl, probably a spotted eagle owl, flopped from concealment among the roots and flew silently along the river bank, soliciting alarm calls en route; it was then I realized my heart was beating heavily. I looked back at the duiker just in time to catch its rear end slipping back into the bush, the hornbill was preening, seemingly oblivious to the drama it had caused.

Duiker. mara river crossing. with owl and hornbill in waterside vegetation

Spotted Eagle Owl
(Bubo africanus)

Elsamere, Naivasha, Kenya.

12½" × 17" (318 × 432mm) Tempera on Arches

It was a perfect day; the sun was shining, a gentle breeze from the lake wafted aromas to and fro and bird song proliferated, punctuated by the periodic call of the fish eagles. I was sitting on the lawn under the canopy of the large yellow acacias that surround the grounds and border the lake at Elsamere, the home of the late Joy Adams. It was an hour or so until lunch and I was catching up on notes and sketching.

I took a break to observe a troop of black and white colobus monkeys that were making their way through the canopy. Focusing my binoculars on the large male leading the way, who had paused to allow the others to catch up, I noticed a large 'blob' amongst the finer tangle of branches, just a metre or so in front of the approaching troop. It turned out to be an owl, a large one. I got up to get a better view and identify it. I had been told that a resident Verreaux's eagle owl had often been seen and heard around the grounds; could this be it? I referred to my book but the verdict was not conclusive.

I watched with bated breath as the troop began to move again. It seemed from below as if they were on a collision course; I was full of anticipation as the monkeys approached the bird one by one – the leader, young males, females and mothers carrying young. But nothing happened, and I can only assume either that they were both familiar with such encounters or that they were further apart than they appeared.

During lunch I met a pleasant young couple who were visiting Elsamere. Bobby had expressed a keen interest in birds, so I enthusiastically related the incident I had just witnessed. Ali exclaimed that she had once kept owls and would love to see the one in the acacia. I agreed to show them the spot after lunch and if it was still there we might be able to positively identify it. It was still there and after much deliberation, we agreed that it was a spotted eagle owl rather than the resident Verreaux's eagle owl.

Bateleur and Buffalo
(Terathopius ecaudatus and Syncerus caffer)

Sweetwaters Tented Camp and Ol'Pejeta Ranch, Kenya.

18" × 24" (457 × 610mm) Oil on Canvas

It was while driving along a dusty track on Ol'Pejeta heading for Sweetwaters Tented Camp that I noticed a large bird way ahead looking as if it was feeding, maybe on a road casualty. It took flight and, as I approached the spot, was flapping away across the plain, struggling to gain height.

I searched the area briefly, hoping to find the reason why it was there; nothing appeared obvious. However, a few yards further on there was a bleached buffalo skull. As I examined it, the bird I had disturbed moments before was gracefully soaring low overhead and from its distinctive shape could be identified as a bateleur eagle, one of Africa's most dramatic birds of prey. I watched it for a while as it turned in great silent arcs, its angles changing with the deft manipulation of its almost non-existent tail and the sun periodically illuminating its powerful colouring. Then the breeze took it over my head and far off into the distance. I turned to resume my journey and as I did so a pair of cisticolas (wren-like birds) flew low and fast across the track, uttering calls of annoyance before disappearing into rough grass. I paused with binoculars at the ready, hoping for a better look, but they did not oblige.

While carrying on my journey to Sweetwaters the idea for the picture developed. Although I did not actually see the scene depicted, I did think that maybe it was the buffalo skull that had caught the attention of the eagle just as it had done mine!

All I needed now was some storm clouds, and a strong source of light to create a dramatic picture, fitting for such a bird. I included Mount Kenya in the background to give location to the event.

Baobab and Hornbill
(Tockus erythrophynchus)

Selous Game Reserve, Tanzania.

15" × 24" (380 × 610mm) Oil on Canvas

The baobab tree is a wonder of the arboreal world. Although I had seen one or two from a distance at Bamburi, it was not until I spent some time in the Selous Game Reserve that I came into close contact with them; in fact the main reception area of Mbuyu Camp, where I was staying, was built around one, giving me a great opportunity to study it at leisure.

Baobabs' shape, form and size can vary enormously, but when one comes across a truly huge specimen one just has to spend time exploring it, it is so interesting. They become host to many animals, from the myriads of insects to reptiles, and large animals such as leopards, set up home in them, playing a vital role in the ecosystems of the areas where they are found. The one I viewed had a bees' nest the size of a dustbin slung under one of the upper branches and bore many scars caused by the attentions of elephants and their destructive tusks.

The tree I chose to paint was encountered on a day trip from Mbuyu to Beho-Beho Camp. It was a particularly magnificent specimen, being solitary and set in a vast area of sand with white whistling thorn bushes interspersed with acacia trees behind and the blue hue of the distant hills beyond.

I introduced the hornbill to give the tree animation and to represent all the other forms of life that may exist among its form. Although the red-billed hornbill, is not native to this area, I used artistic licence because I wanted a 'hat' of red to act as a focal point, and attract one's eye to the impala buck which may have otherwise been overlooked. When the antelope is noticed, the scale of the tree becomes obvious.

This picture is one of a group of more 'genteel' landscapes which act as an antidote to the ones containing dead animals, skulls and dark skies. I make no excuses for these paintings; we all need compromise and contrast in whatever form it comes.

Yellow-Billed Hornbills
(Tockus flavirostris)

Selous Game Reserve, Tanzania.

9" × 13" (229 × 330mm) Watercolour on Arches

These studio studies were worked up from field sketches and notes made while observing a single bird in an acacia thicket at Mbuyu Camp. At one point the bird dropped from its perch in what was a half-hearted attempt at catching a gecko; the gecko scampered for cover seemingly none the worse for its experience.

While I was sketching, a small herd of zebra came down to the water's edge to drink, nervous and alert as always, through fear of ambush.

Yellow Billed Hornbill
"Tockus flavirostris"

Selous G. R. Tanzania '95

White-Fronted Bee-Eater
(Merops bullockoides)

Hell's Gate National Park, Naivasha, Kenya.

11" × 14" (279 × 356mm) Oil on Canvas

Around Naivasha the white-fronted bee-eater seems to predominate, although other members of the family are seen on occasions. This one was drawn while my guide, Henry Ndede, and I were having a rest after spending the morning walking in the Hell's Gate National Park just a few miles south of Naivasha. The gully that we had been exploring was a type of sandstone and was used for the backdrop for this picture. The beautiful, warm ochre colour was a perfect complement to the bird's plumage, with the soft green of the vine leaves contrasting with the iridescent green of the bird's back.

We were up early and at the park before dawn. We had seen some leopard tracks by the car park the previous day and were informed by the local warden that the cats passed by regularly just after dawn. Not having had a good look at leopards in the wild, I thought this would be a good opportunity and persuaded Henry to come along. The morning was cold and dark; the sun was not quite up, still having to surmount the surrounding hills. Mornings like these are seldom a waste of time; even though the cats did not show up it was worth it for the dawn chorus. Listening to the African bush wake up is always a wonderful experience.

Later on that morning Henry found a dead yellow white-eye, a small yellowish-green warbler-type bird, in perfect condition, which I took back to draw. I made two quite detailed sketches of it later that afternoon and left it on the patio with the intention of painting it the following morning. When I returned to resume my work, however, I was shocked to find a mass of black ants where the bird had been. On closer inspection I found the legs, empty head and a few feathers. I shall be more careful where I leave things in future!

yellow white eye.
'Zosterops senegalensis'
found by Henry Ndede while walking
in the 'Ol Njorowa' gorge Hells Gate Naivasha.
and drawn by me shortly afterwards.

little Be-Eaters,
White fronted Be-Eaters

" HELLS GATE NAIVASHA "

Great White Egret
(Egretta alba)

Baobab Farm, Bamburi, Kenya.

8½" × 12½" (216 × 318mm) Watercolour

What made this incident immediately appealing was the simple but dramatic sense of dark and light. I was watching the egret stalking the lilypads for some time, before it wandered into a position where it and some of the lilies were in full sunlight. The luminosity and brilliance of the bird's plumage, the vibrant lime green of the lily leaves interspersed with the delicate mauve of the blooms and the reflection, all set against a very dark backdrop, made for a theatrical experience.

My only regret was that I did not draw the picture twice the size

Selous Kudu
(*Tregelaphus strepsiceros*)

Selous Game Reserve, Tanzania

14" × 20" (356 × 508mm) Oil on Canvas

While flying over the Selous Game Reserve, Tanzania to Mbuyu Camp where I was to spend the next month, the contrast to the Mara was obvious. Gone were the myriad of criss-crossing car tracks caused by off road safari vechicles, replaced by the more gentle single meanderings caused by elephants and game. The area was vast, wild and with almost no sign of human habitation. From the air, small groups of hippos and elephants could be seen drinking and wallowing in the many waterways that segmented the bush.

It was on landing at the small dirt airstrip by the camp that the true nature of the place became apparent. It was hot, the air still lightly scented and pure, everything was bleached in the mid afternoon sun, a sense of untamed isolation pervaded the scene. Greetings with the camp manager, Sal, were exchanged and we headed for Mbuyu.

It was during the short drive to the camp, when apart from a single wart-hog, I encountered my first Greater kudu. I gestured to stop, but Sal assured me I would see many more, and as the other guests were keen to make 'camp' he was right; I too made the most of the comfort on offer.

I did encounter many of these beautiful and majestic animals during my stay but they never lingered long, once one stopped to observe them in detail, melting into the bush that conceals them so totally.

"Termite mounds" Selous Game Reserve – Tanzania.
"Greater Kudu" Mbuyu camp

Pied Kingfisher and Crocodile
(Ceryle rudis and Crocodylus niloticus)

Selous Game Reserve, Tanzania.

11" × 14" (279 × 356mm) Oil on Canvas

Pied kingfishers must be some of the most numerous and successful of their species. Wherever there is a stretch of suitable water, be it stream, river, lake or even coastline, these birds were to be found – not just in ones and twos but at times numbering a dozen or more.

I remember observing an area at the most southerly tip of Lake Naivasha known as the Hippo Pool. There there were numerous dead trees standing in the water and around the lake shore and each one seemed to have a resident bird. I watched one bird which had just caught a fish, probably a tilarpia or black bass, settle on a branch to feed. It bashed the fish against the branch before turning it so that it would go down head first before attempting to swallow it. The fish seemed to be just a little too large, so it repeated the bashing and juggling before trying again, but still no luck. This routine went on for a good 20 minutes, with the kingfisher's frustration becoming more and more obvious until it finally dropped the fish and with a look of disdain and a harsh call flew off. The fish, bobbing in the swell belly up, made easy pickings for a passing egret.

The two kingfishers in the painting were observed at Mbuyu Camp on the banks of a tributary to the Rufiji river in the Selous Game Reserve. They were not in a feeding mood and were content to relax and preen on a perch just above the water. As I watched from my 'perch' on the river bank I noticed a shadowy shape moving just below the surface. I could not make out what it was and assumed it was a fish. It was not until it came closer and gently surfaced without so much as a ripple, that I realised it was a small crocodile about 40cm long. The birds, which were only about two metres away, took no notice.

Although I found out later that crocodiles were very common in these sand rivers and subsequently saw many of them, of all sizes, this was my first truly wild one and filled me with excitement.

I often saw greenshank, plovers and sandpipers sharing the same small sand bars with crocodiles as they sunbathed.

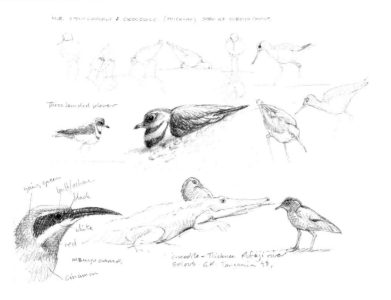

Rhino and Cattle Egrets (Savannah Siesta)
(Ceratotherum simum and Ardeola ibis)

16" × 20" (406 × 508mm) Acrylic on Board

This painting was completed in 1991 and donated to the "Whaletail" exhibition, Nairobi, Kenya, in aid of the East African Wildlife Society.

Although not actually part of the 'Birds and Beasts' project, I thought the subject matter more than appropriate to include in this book.

I had little luck with rhinos in the wild during my three months, however, I did manage to observe a black rhino 'Morani' at Ol'Pejeta Ranch which was orphaned and under twenty-four hour guard. Another opportunity occurred while staying at the Mara Safari Club, where not far away there were two white rhinos (the subject of the painting) being looked after before being released into the Mara to boost the local population. They were brought in from South Africa where the anti-poaching methods are effective and as a result the populations are strong and stable, creating a surplus which can be used for rehabilitation projects elsewhere in Africa.

The main difference between the black and white rhino is their eating habits; the black being a browser, taking a selection of vegetation from bushes and shrubs above ground, and has a pointed upper lip to enable it to pick the leaves; the white rhino is a grazer and has a wide square lip in common with other herbivores that graze grass. The word white is probably a derivation of 'wide' describing its mouth.

After the Rain

Masai Mara, Kenya.

15" × 25" (380 × 635mm) Oil on Canvas

I have seen double rainbows on a few occasions over the Marlborough Downs from my studio window in England, but somehow this one was brighter and larger, in keeping with its vast setting. I noticed, after a while, that the sky on the outside of the rainbow was a few degrees darker than that on the inside and that the colour orders of the two bands were reversed. I made notes of my observations and felt compelled to record them in this picture.

As the storm subsided and drifted away over the Aitong Hills, the sun came out and created a striking colour combination: the rich orange ochre of the vast savannah made fresher and brighter by the recent rains against the blue-grey hue of the distant hills, not quite free of rain and dark cloud. and dissected by a brilliant double rainbow.

With the passing of the rain came the increased activities of the resident masked weaver birds as the males resumed their nest-building chores and courtship displays. The tree, containing the colony of about 50 nests, came alive as the yellow and black attire of the males flashed in the bright sun. A lone cheetah, bedraggled from the storm, wandered forlornly across the plain in contrast to the vibrant activity of the birds, with the vanguard of the wildebeest migration looking on.

Adolescence

Masai Mara, Kenya.

18" × 24" (457 × 610mm) Oil on Canvas

We came across an area of burning grass, the large black area smoking and logs smouldering, the flames at the leading edge being fanned by the breeze and devouring all in their path. There were several birds hawking the flame line, catching the insects as they fled. I got very excited by the ideas the situation was offering me: the black scorched earth, the wisps of smoke, and the licking flames that crackled, popped and spat their way through the grass, with the phoenix-like rollers dancing in and out of the fire and ashes.

I worked hard and made several preliminary sketches, but could not finalise things – they just would not gel. Although the idea still excites me and I am keen to do a full painting containing all aspects of that episode, for now it has been put on the back-burner.

As a consolation I have used two of the rollers to animate what was becoming a monochrome event – the adolescent male lion needed an incident to waken him up, the picture needing something to brighten it.

The Masai herdsmen practice the tradition of burning small areas of grassland to encourage new growth for their cattle, like the gamekeepers of northern England and Scotland who burn heather to encourage new shoots for the grouse.

Bright Future (Lion Cub)
(Panthera Leo)

Masai Mara, Kenya.

8" × 10" (203 × 254mm) Oil on Board

As mentioned before 'lion watching' was always a joy, to be an observer of these truly noble beasts in their natural surroundings at such close quarters stirred my emotions and excited the heart, whether they were lazing in the afternoon heat around the remains of their last meal or ambling across the plains in the cool of the evening preparing for a night-time hunt, one always felt privileged and on edge never knowing what could happen, and being totally out of control.

Very often a pride would be located relaxing on raised ground amongst scrub and boulders, surprisingly well hidden and easily missed even when passing just metres away; sometimes just the flick of a tail or the twitch of an ear would reveal the presence of another, concealed amongst the grass; what often started out as a group of three or four could grow to double figures with such revelations. I found it a great exercise in observation to scan the surrounding undergrowth with binoculars, looking for the nearest clue to betray the lie of another. I found one half-grown individual in the thickest of cover just by the regular swelling of its flank as it dozed contentedly. The cub in the painting was unaccounted for until it raised its head and caught the sun. It viewed my presence with disdain.

The lions' range and numbers are declining due to the ever-increasing pressure and demands of the expanding human population all over East Africa. However, in the larger game reserves such as the Masai Mara in Kenya and the Serengetti in Tanzania their numbers seem stable and they can look forward to a 'Bright Future'.

Simba Cub

Masai Mara, Kenya.

9½" × 13½" (241 × 343mm) Tempera on Arches

'Cute', 'sweet' and 'twee', are not words that readily come to mind when describing many of the pictures in this book, but one could be excused for using them in this case.

This picture was painted as a preliminary work for a much larger one (possibly with the cub life-size), keeping it simple in content, with muted foliage contrasting with the soft glow and warm hue of the morning sun, perhaps with the inclusion of a small bird.

Lion cub "soaking up the sun" Masai-Mara Aug 93
"contemplating."

Black Stork
(*Ciconia nigra*)

9" × 13" (229 × 330mm) Acrylic on Board

Although not resident in the Masai Mara, during their migration from Europe one can expect to see black storks at any time, and in situations such as 'storking' pools left by a sudden rainstorm, wooded areas and along the Mara river.

This individual was sat hunched by the side of a pool which had been replenished by a passing storm. It was the only one I saw during my stay and given the time of year, late August, I thought myself lucky, as it was unusually early for such arrivals.

At one point it shook itself vigorously, shedding the water from its feathers and as the halo of droplets disappeared, it regained its pose. Neck and breast feathers then gently enveloped its powerful red beak as its head sank between its shoulders, creating a somewhat unusual but beautiful form – an interesting sculpture.

Black Stork.
"Ciconia niga"
observed at small
Pond by Lake Nakuru.
(Probably an escapee).
(normally a European
bird).

Lion Male
(Panthero leo)

18" × 26" (457 × 660mm) Tempera on Arches

When watching these magnificent beasts at close quarters in the wild one gets a feel for the strength, power and prowess they possess; despite the fact that they seem to spend 75 per cent of their time lying around and dozing, it is still there under the surface.

   These two drawings in tempera were an exploration of form and texture, a search for what was lying just below the surface – one always had to take them seriously!

Lion Male
(Panthera leo)

18½" × 26" (470 × 660mm) Tempera on Arches

"Simba"
Masai Mara Aug 93

"Simba" Masai Mara Aug 94.

Oryx
(Oryx gazella)

Baobab Farm, Bamburi, Kenya.

8½" × 12½" (222 × 318mm) Tempera on Arches

These studies were made around the same time as the eland mother and calf pictures (page 8). As well as the resident herd of eland there were oryx, which were free to roam a vast area of bush. During the day they are difficult to find, but, I was told by one of the rangers that at about 5 pm they came back for feeding and passed by the car park.

I sat on a very large fossilized giant clam and waited. The first thing I noticed was the clouds of dust drifting on the breeze, glowing orange from being backlit by the setting sun, then the javelin-type horns and finally the animals themselves. It was a large herd, about 30 or so animals from very small babies to fully grown bulls, and they came wafting past like cattle to the milking parlour.

Oryx Bayobab Farm
(Bamburi Mombasa)

"ORYX." "oryx gazella"

Baobab farm, Mombasa.

Motherhood – Mother with Cubs
(Panthera Leo)

Masai Mara, Kenya.

8" × 10" (203 × 254mm) Oil on Board

She was powerful, genteel, caring, contented and in her prime; all these words came to mind as I watched this particular female suckling her cubs.

She was the biggest and most handsome lioness I had come across, a fine example and testament to the conditions and easy living she found in the Masai Mara.

For the thirty minutes or so of my time observing and sketching her, she barely stirred, just gently nuzzling and licking her cubs on occasions, as they jostled for positions. The scene was one of total peace, tolerance and acceptance.

Although the situations could not be more opposed, one could not help comparing the scene in front of me with a litter of kittens in a hay barn or an attentive labrador suckling her pups on a hearth-rug.

Despite domestication, evolution and the passage of time creating a vast gulf between the two realities, common ground is still there in abundance.

The Intruder – Lioness and Cubs
(*Panthera Leo*)

Selous Game Reserve, Tanzania.

24" × 36" (610 × 914mm) Oil on Canvas

It was one of those perfect afternoons, not too hot and with a gentle breeze; we were meandering through the parched undergrowth which bordered the many large expanses of water, typical of this part of the Selous. We had heard earlier from a previous traveller that a pride of lions were in the vicinity and were feeding on a fresh kill.

We approached the spot with anticipation but alas no sign of them; were we in the right place or had they moved on? We searched the area thoroughly, well as thoroughly as one can from the safety of a vehicle, albeit open-topped, but to no avail, we decided to move on. We had gone just a few hundred yards and as we rounded a bend, wow! there they were, just off the track resting amongst the bush, and quite a gathering; two large males, several females and many cubs, all lazing around the remains of a wildebeest. Well the adults were resting, eyes opening briefly to register our intrusion, before closing again, mouths agape and panting heavily, looking as though nothing could shift them.

As for the cubs, they seemed oblivious to the heat and their full stomachs, always looking for something to do. Stalking the tail of an adult and pouncing when it periodically moved, wrestling with it at one end while its owner slept at the other. There was the odd snarl and snap of indignation from an adult to warn a cub it had overstepped the mark, otherwise they were remarkably tolerant; one cub in particular took great delight in using the remains of the wildebeest as a climbing frame, clambering over its horns and hanging from the exposed rib-cage, on occasions stopping to check whether we were still watching. We were; after one such check, he disappeared inside the carcass, the stretched skin began to distort and move, resembling a hapless camper inside a collapsing tent. Goodness knows what he was doing in there, but he emerged several moments later, looking very pleased with himself.

Pearl Spotted Owlet
(Glaucidium perlatum)

Selous Game Reserve, Tanzania.

8" × 10" (203 × 254mm) Oil on Canvas

It was while on a day trip with Will and Camilla, a honeymoon couple from England, that I first encountered this small owl. It was sitting in the peripheral branches of an acacia tree, seemingly staring back at us with large black eyes. It was not until I approached it for a better look that it turned its head through 180 degrees revealing two bright yellow eyes, the two 'eyes' I had seen at first were just black markings on the back of the head, but very convincing.

One of the reasons for the trip was to visit Selous' Grave. Captain Frederic Courteney Selous, DSO was a pioneer, explorer, naturalist, hunter and conservationist. While serving with the 25th Royal Fusiliers, fighting the Germans under General von Lettow-Vorbeck, he was killed on 4 January 1917. He gave his life and name to a very special part of Africa.

On reaching his grave, a simple stone slab with a bronze plaque, I stood in the searing heat contemplating his fate. There was very little sound apart from the occasional hum of an insect. It dawned on me that the surrounding area probably had not changed for many thousands of years, let alone the 80 years since his death.

Pearl-Spotted Owlet
(Glaucidium perlatum)

large black spots
resemble 'eyes' from
behind

Buffalo skull with
catapillar crysatists
whch feed on the
horn covering.

Selous Game Reserve.

O Lord of love and kindness, who
created the beautiful earth and all the
creatures walking and flying in it,
so that they may proclaim your glory,
I thank you to my dying day that
you have placed me amongst them.
Francis of Assisi